TRUE TALES OF THREE STEERS

True Tales of Three Steers

MENTORO, BRAVANDO, and
IMPPO
with
BEAUVENA HEIFFER
and
BEAU BUMLY

by

JOHN CORNELIUS SHERBNO

A Fairy-Philosophical Tale
A Children's Tale for Adults
An Adult's Tale for Children

PHILOSOPHICAL LIBRARY
New York

Library of Congress Catalog Card No. 76-169245
SBN 8022-2062-2

. . . Such Symbolic Consciousness was to the Christian Community (as It is to Every Man) the First Attempt of His Consciousness of Self, . . . World, . . . God to find Its way back to Its Original Unity and express Its discoveries along that arduous Way. But . . . above all, the man of symbolic consciousness does not recognize his Self-consciousness as symbolic. He continues to judge the Ultimate meaningfulness of all Events and all Truths by their direct relationship to himself.

Adapted from: P. 46 (and 213), David Tracy, *The Achievement of Bernard Lonergan.*

TABLE OF CONTENTS

INTRODUCTION

The Dedication and Preface

For personal reasons (all his own)

the Author wishes to dedicate this trial to Himself, and to preface it with the remark: ". . . that it is a serious effort at telling a children's tale in the language of adults, yet at the same time at telling an adult's tale in the language of children." Therefore, what he has written down within these pages is not worth a hill of jelly beans, but what is important and may be worth a hill of beans—jellied or otherwise—is what the Reader understands, for the success or failure of this work depends upon the Reader's understanding of it, more than upon what the Author has written down.

Finally, Every Person views reality through their own windows, yet often another (especially, if one is blind to some realities) lights up the unseen way ahead. With this idea in mind, the Author humbly dines on crow pies in acknowledging Candle Bearers: Tanta, EEK, The Wolf, Injun Joe, The Group, The Captain, The Princess, The Little One, The Sarg and His Nurse, The Nurse, The Hospital and lesser but not least of all: thirteen of the most fearsome—they indeed could put fear into the fearless heart of a St. George, fire-eating, smoke-belching, noise-making, mountainous-molehill wreckers, etc., etc., and etc. Little Daemon-

Dragons-Monsters this side of birth, yet without which and the likes of which the Author would still be in the dark about many of life's brighter moments of despair, of frustration, and of irreality. Now in conclusion, lest The Reader not think that he—The Author—was 'all at sea' when writing this saga, the following historical "N.B." is appended: this final manuscript for revision put out to sea with a ketch, weathered many a stormy hour and day, but came about to a safe harbor aboard the *El Yen Maru.* . . .

26 May 1967
Wakeman, Ohio

P.S.—Vota meo Domino reddam.
     Coram omni populo eius. (ps. 115)

Acknowledgment

Grateful thanks are due to Herder and Herder, Inc., for permission to quote from their excellent publication: Tracy, David, *The Achievement of Bernard Lonergan* (New York: Herder and Herder, Inc., 1971).

TRUE TALES OF THREE STEERS

CHAPTER ONE

The One Steer Symphony Orchestra

Once upon a not so very long ago, and in a place not so very far from here, Beauvena and Imppo gave a concert. It did not start out quite that way. In fact it really started a long way away out West in the Symphonic Grotto, but because we must start these *True Tales of Three Steers* some-place, we'll start with the story of a concert that almost didn't take place, and which when it did take place took place many years "afterwards" when they were on their way back from the Orient.

It all began when the Loco Weed Gang and Beau Bumly, alias, "The Bum Steer," tried to kidnap the symphony or-chestra of one hundred and forty-nine musicians, the con-ductor, and Beauvena, and they would have succeeded except for Imppo and Bravando. But the kidnaping was not the only big news story that day, as an even bigger one was the very surprising concert that did take place.

Beauvena Heiffer, who is the loveliest of cows—indeed she won for several years in a row, "The Miss Bovine of America Contest"—had a beautiful singing voice, as well. One of her sharpest critics wrote, ". . . this corn fed rose with the creamy complexion has a most mellow quality in singing, but especially in her low tones . . . ." She was in love with Imppo and she knew that he loved her, even though he had never said so, for he was forever mooning over her and look-ing at her with those big greenish-brown calf eyes of his.

Truly Imppo was shy. In fact he is very shy, and especially so when Beauvena is nearby. So shy in fact that he not only blushes red all over, but in other colors as well. He even glows like a glow worm. He even flashes more rapidly, than a neon sign and looks for all the world like a theatre marquee all lit up for an opening night. Of course, this is all right, if you are a glow worm or a theatre marquee, but it is most embarrassing if you are a very young steer, which is just what Imppo is.

Imppo is quite musical, too, a talent that he and Beauvena discovered by accident one day some years ago in a curious way in the Symphonic Grotto, which is at one end of The Plaid Moonbow Gulch, which is at one end of The Hidden Valley, which is at one end of The One Way Tunnel, which is at one end of The Up Only Trail, which goes up The Steepest Side of The Tallest Mountain nearby their home away out West.

The kidnaping, which was staged by Beau Bumly, alias, "The Bum Steer," and the Loco Weed Gang, took place as Beauvena was nearing the end of a world concert tour, and as the little group of friends were returning home from the Far East.

The very famous midwestern symphony orchestra had booked Beauvena for a special concert. Indeed, an honor for them both. The famous conductor as was his custom called a brief rehearsal for full orchestra, the soloist, and himself, the evening before the concert. It was to be held "on stage" and not downstairs in the Practice Room, for he wished a dress rehearsal, as well. The conductor also ordered that guards be stationed at all of the doors leading into the concert hall, so that no one would interrupt their practice session. These preparations almost led to tragic results, for the stagehands and electricians were sent home and were told to return the next day, so that they might clean-up and set-up the stage and lighting for the concert. They grumbled about this, for it meant a rushed job just before the night's concert. Also, the guards were especially watchful that no one entered for the Concert Hall Manager had told them that if any reporters or unwelcomed "gatecrashers" were found in the hall watching or listening to the secret rehearsal, he would fire them on the spot. What no one suspected was that one of the trusted guards was a member of The Loco Weed Gang. It was he who was to open the door for the kidnaping.

Just about twenty hours before concert time, the Assistant Manager, who was always checking things in the Concert Hall, came running and yelling into the Manager's Office. He was yelling so loudly and was so very excited that the Manager could not understand just what it was that he was trying to say, so he tried to quiet him down. When he understood what it was that he was trying to tell him then the Assistant Manager had to try to quiet him down.

"But-t-t-t-t, it can't be true!" cried the Manager. "It never has happened before, why should it happen now and to me? It didn't, did it?"

"It did," was the Assistant Manager's reply, "and here's the ransom note." But in his excitement, he had forgotten which hand held the ransom note and which held his handkerchief, so he was mopping his forehead with the ransom note and waving his handkerchief under the eyes of his Manager. The Manager grabbed the damp wrinkled torn ransom note and read it:

> *"We've kidnaped the orchestra, the conductor and Beauvena, and we want $10,000,000.00 in large bills before we return them in time for tomorrow's concert."*

The note was signed by the leader of the Loco Weed Gang, Beau Bumly, alias, "The Bum Steer."

"It-t-t-t-t can't-t-t be," he said. Then realizing that it was true, he ran out of his Office, down the hallway, past the doors of the many practice rooms, up the UPSTAIRWAY, down another long hallway, and out onto the empty concert stage, where he (and the Assistant Manager, who had followed close behind) expected to find the practicing musicians, but where they did not find: Beauvena, nor the Conductor, nor the orchestra of one hundred and forty-nine musicians. All they did find was the Conductor's broken baton, Beauvena's crushed flowers, and one hundred and forty-nine chairs and music stands either overturned or pushed aside, as if a furious struggle had taken place.

"They've really been kidnaped," the Manager and Assistant Manager said together in a duet.

"Call the police," he cried, "and be sure to call the newspapers." And then the Manager promptly fainted right there on stage, just nineteen hours and thirty minutes before concert time. But the Assistant Manager did not call the police, nor the newspapers, as just nineteen hours and twenty-nine minutes and ten seconds before concert time, he too fainted right there on stage, and this is where they were found the next day, just ten hours before concert time, when the guards admitted the stagehands and electricians into the hall. The Chief Electrician read the ransom note and immediately called the police, just nine hours and forty-five minutes before concert time.

The Chief-of-Police had listened to the improbable story of the Chief Electrician and then he immediately telephoned the two heads of the FIB and AIC, and then all three of them called the newspapers. Later, about eight hours and twelve minutes before concert time, the Chief-of-Police re-read for the hundredth time to the crime reporters the contents of the ransom note, and pointed out that it was signed with the DEADHEAD SEAL of the Loco Weed Gang, so that there was no doubt about "who done it." (As one reporter described it, The DEADHEAD SEAL was: a shrunken skull of a dead ox with two broken long horns framed inside of two sets of double crossed double jointed leg bones, so that one set was over the horns and the other set under the sunken chin.) Also the Chief had told the Manager to get in touch with Beauvena's nearest friends or relatives, ". . . just in case . . ."

As the Cub reporters holding onto the hastily scribbled notes of the more experienced crime reporters ran for the door, to get the story to their editors, Beauvena's three friends, The Three Steers: Mentoro, Bravando, and Imppo came rushing blindly into the hall—through the same doorway! They met with an awful head-on crash. Little slips of note paper flew in every direction for a fair-thee-well. (This explains in part why the first news accounts of the "kidnaping" or "the alleged kidnaping" or "the supposed kidnaping" were so confusing.) But soon the "EXTRAS" were on the city's streets and when the newsboys sold the late late edition the general public learned that the concert scheduled for that evening had been called off just five hours and two minutes before concert time.

Despite their noisy entrance, the Chief-of-Police was happy to see The Three Steers, well, almost all three. He was glad to have Mentoro around to advise him, as he could think like the gangsters. Also Bravando would be very handy in a fight, of which he had many and never lost any. But that Imppo, well, that was a horse, or, a steer of another color. Anyone could see that he was just not cut out for police work. It wasn't only that his legs were wobbly, but they even were uneven, while all of the time his shaggy-nappy hair kept catching on things, like: the music stands which as they toppled over sailed their sheets of music all over the place; or that tall delicately balanced bell chime rack, which when it fell, knocked over two kettledrums and the nearby cymbals—one xylophone, and one graceful harp, and just missed the bullroarers on its way down the platform steps. Indeed it must be admitted that never in the long history of the Concert Hall had any cacodemon ever caused such cacophony. But just when the Chief-of-Police and the Manager were about to throw him out on his horns and tail, Imppo began to glow.

"Look, Bravando," whispered Mentoro, "Imppo's got his 'Trail Light' on, I s'pose he's onto Beauvena's trail," and sure enough he was, for a trail of footprints began to appear in the bright footlights of the stage.

When Imppo really began to glow, the Chief Electrician, who didn't know about Imppo and his very unusual lighting ability, yelled, "Turn off those crazy colored lights, or you'll burn out all my fuses." But Mentoro had spoken to the Chief-of-Police about Imppo and he changed that order by commanding, "Turn out the house lights, he works better in the dark. I s'pose!" and immediately all of the lights in the concert hall were turned out and all that could now be seen was the beaming Imppo, who began to glow brighter and brighter as more and more of Beauvena's footsteps began to appear in the dark.

Footprints were running all over the stage and it was some time before the Police Division for Identification of Finger-and-Foot Prints was able to sort them out. After all, trying to find just three hundred and four particular footprints in all of those thousands of prints that could by now be seen was no easy job, even for experts. But Imppo had immediately spotted Beauvena's foot prints "down stage far right" and began to follow them as they left the stage and went towards the DOWNSTAIRWAY.

Bravando nudged Mentoro, and then went off after Imppo to be nearby "just in case" he needed help sudden-like. Mentoro again spoke to the Chief-of-Police, who upon learning that Imppo was going off stage and towards the DOWN-STAIRWAY, blew his police whistle and ordered his men to follow him and "that disappearing Trail Light." Now what happened in the next few minutes in the darkened musical concert hall has never before been revealed to the light of day, but happen it did—unfortunately.

Mentoro reached the DOWNSTAIRWAY just after Imppo and Bravando disappeared down it (he could still see Imppo's glow and Bravando's fearsome shadow) but just ahead of the Chief-of-Police, who was just ahead of the two Heads of the FIB and AIC, who were just ahead of the manager and Assistant Manager, who were just barely ahead of the army of policemen, newspaper reporters, photographers, stagehands, and electricians. Now, all of this would have been fine and no real story at all, except for one unexpected happening that upset everything, or everyone: Mentoro tripped over the bottom of his too long of a robe right at the top step of the DOWNSTAIRWAY, and in the dark.

For a fact, just as he reached the top of the DOWN-STAIRWAY, Mentoro tripped, and then the Chief-of-Police, who was following too closely, tripped over Mentoro. Then the two Heads of the FIB and the AIC tripped over them. Then the Manager and Assistant Manager tripped over all four. AND THEN the whole army of policemen, newspaper reporters and photographers, stagehands and electricians, all tripped over the six of them. With arms and legs flying, cameras and pencils sailing through the air, hammers and screw drivers soaring here and there, amidst yells in the dark, the whole mess went heels over heads down the DOWN-STAIRWAY like a giant ball of very loose spaghetti. They all hit the bottom step with a giant "THUD-QUISH" and finally looking very much like a cookie thin oozy uncooked pancake slid across the hallway and against the far wall with a loud "SQUAWAKISHNESS."

Meanwhile, Imppo and Bravando were far down that same hallway watching the footprints disappear under the door marked:

PRACTICE ROOM #1

ORCHESTRA ONLY

"She's in there, Bravando, but watch out, so are Bumly and the rest." And then Imppo stepped to one side to let his brother go by, for Bravando had a running start and when he hit that locked-bolted-barred-barricaded sound proof door with only his left shoulder, it crumbled as if it were an old loose rusty screen backdoor.

Into the Practice Room thundered Bravando with Imppo right behind him, The Loco Weed Gang froze with fear at the explosive entrance and the unexpected discovery (they thought that no one would ever look for them right under the scene of the crime), but they quickly thawed out under the fiery tempers of the two rescuers and of Beau Bumly, and of the rising heat of the hot battle that followed their sudden discovery. When Bumly turned out the lights, so that he could sneak off in the dark with Beauvena still a captive, Imppo turned up his special emergency glow-beams away-beyond the danger point and lit up the whole Practice Room #1, as if it were high noon on the sun. Then with a bounding lopsided lope and a quick "one-here" and a "two-there" combination punch, all of the flight and fight went out of Bumly. Meanwhile, Bravando was enjoying himself, what with only four or five of the gangsters piling on at a time, he almost got bored with the whole affair. But soon there weren't any more to pile on, for what with the number that he had speared with his horns and tossed over his shoulders or those that ran into his solid iron-like sides in the darkened room, the fight was soon over. Indeed, they had fought so fiercely and so well, that when the Chief-of-Police (and all) arrived, at last, looking the worse for their fall, the short battle was all over and there was little left to do but round up the moaning and groaning kidnapers and cart them off to the pen. In fact, the only real struggle going on in the Practice Room was between Imppo and Beauvena, for she was hugging and hugging him, while he was trying to escape her tight clutches. That he was embarrassed you could tell from the way he kept glowing and glowing and glowing.

Finally, after the Lawmen had rawhided the Loco Weed Gang off to jail and all of the reporters and photographers had returned back to their papers, except one or two who had hung around to see the outcome, the Manager decided that there was still time to prepare for the concert and keep up their cherished tradition of "the show must go on" no matter what. He told this to the remaining reporters and they too left with the good news.

Happily the Manager with the help of the Assistant Manager began to untie the Conductor and all of the one hundred and forty-nine waiting musicians. But then just fifty-six minutes before concert time, the Manager let out a shrill, "YIIIIIIiiiii" that turned, churned and rendered all of their hearts into melted butter. Quickly they went to see what troubled him now.

"There still can't be a concert, tonight. We shoulda paid the ransom! Quick call back the reporters and tell them." And then he fainted.

"But," asked the Chief-of-Police, who had stayed for the concert and whose knowledge of music and musical instruments was limited to the number of notes he could blow on his police whistle, "we've found your orchestra, the conductor, and Beauvena, why not? now?"

The Assistant Manager began mopping his brow—for he never could stand it when some one fainted in a practice room—explained to the Chief-of-Police, "Look at them!" and the Chief looked. "They've been tied up for such a long time that none of them can move an arm or leg, a foot or a hand, much less finger an instrument, and there isn't time to get them ready before concert time!" and he started to topple at the thought. For indeed all of the musicians (with the exception of Beauvena) had been tied up so tightly for such a long time that they were now numb and had no feeling at all. "Beau Bumly," cried the Assistant Manager, "has won after all, just as he said he would." And then he too fainted.

Had Beau won? No! For Beauvena had a plan, and it would work, if they would only let her try it, and if Imppo would help her? But of course he would.

She had thought of her plan while being held a captive, when her hands and feet began to grow numb. At that time she had asked Bumly, if he would please untie her, "As they were beginning to hurt." Now Bumly was sorta sweet on her, so he ordered her untied. She had noticed also that the others were becoming numb, and when she couldn't get Bumly to untie them too, she began to worry about what would happen, if help did not come soon. (She always knew Imppo would find her.) But right now, she had to get every one, especially the Manager, The Conductor, and the Orchestra to agree with her. Imppo of course would agree, once she promised him that no one would find out "their secret."

The revived Manager almost fainted again when Beauvena outlined her plan. The Conductor would have no part of it. But then Bravando, who was standing behind Beauvena, kinda sorta unkinda frowned at them, and they quickly nodded both of their heads. So Beauvena began explaining to the waiting stagehands just what to do.

The Practice Room was right under the stage overhead. Also a part of the floor of the Practice Room could be raised or lowered very much like an elevator floor, up through the two large trap doors in the Practice Room's ceiling, or in the floor of the stage, depending upon where you were standing. All of the chairs with the musicians in them were moved onto the "elevator-like floor" and in just the arrangement the Conductor insisted upon the day before. The Conductor, however, kept toppling over when they tried to stand him up at his podium, so they finally had to tie him in a high chair. Then with but just four minutes left before concert time, and with the sounds of the audience overhead hurrying to their seats, Beauvena put into operation the next and most important part of her plan. She told the Chief Electrician to turn all of the light switches on "VERY DIM" (Imppo and she had insisted on this, so that no one would walk about and discover their secret.) Finally with but fifty seconds to go, but still on time, before the scheduled concert, she nodded to the Chief Electrician again, and this time he threw "ON" the switches that began raising the Floor, and with it the Orchestra, the Conductor, and Beauvena, and all one hundred and forty-nine musicians. The trap doors overhead slowly opened to let them through and right up to stage level.

At first, the audience was confused by the dimly lit stage, and the missing orchestra. Perhaps, the newspapers had not gotten the story correct, after all. Then the trap doors opened and the audience knew that they were in for a very unusual and a very fine concert, after such an unusual "overture." They clapped in appreciation. But then just when the tops of the heads of some of the musicians began to appear (the more shiny ones) the cruelest blow of all hit that ill-fated concert. Fuses began blowing out one by one, until finally the electrical load became too great and the MAIN FUSES blew out, finally. This threw the whole hall and audience into darkness.

As soon as the secondary fuses began blowing, the Chief Electrician and his crew began replacing them, but they just could not work fast enough, and also in their hurry some one dropped a box of secondary fuses, and some one else kept getting them mixed up with main fuses, and so the lights kept coming on and going out. Finally they were all in properly and the house lights came on "DIM," as before. Backstage to everyone's great surprise the orchestra, the conductor and Beauvena were all in place and ready for the concert. But how did the stage rise?

Then the Chief Electrician and the Chief Stagehand both saw what had happened. When he first heard the cry for more fuses, Bravando did not wait, he quickly ran under the slowly sinking stage and placed his gigantic shoulders and back against it, stopping it half-way back down, and then began to raise it into place even with the stage level. The quick thinking Chief Stagehand quickly locked the floor into place, for it is doubtful if even Bravando could have held it there throughout the three hour concert.

The audience quieted down, again, as it saw the orchestra sitting there expectantly and so unmovingly, as was the conductor. Only Beauvena was visible to them as she stood there in the baby spotlight. My how radiant she looked! (She was wondering if Imppo had seen the Love-Knot that she wore for him in one of her short dark tresses? A little glow in the corner of her left eye told her that he had so! But he had better be careful about that glowing, or 'their' secret would be discovered before the night was over. He was such a mooncalf, at times!)

Then the concert began. The first notes of the piece:

"The Entrance March of the Brave Bulls," The Overture from the Opera, THE BRAVE BULLS, in which the trumpets and the drums have such magnificent parts, sounded throughout the vast filled hall bringing an electrified hush, a spine-tingling thrill, and in warm human hearts an ecstatic shocking chill of a holiday crowd gathered for an afternoon's kill. The Conductor was so startled that he almost fell from his podium, and would have, except that he was tied to it. Both the Manager and the Assistant Manager almost fainted with sheer pleasure that there was going to be a concert after all. And such music! The one hundred and forty-nine musicians settled back to listen with well-tuned ears to the music they were supposed to be playing. Beauvena was now more in love with Imppo than ever before, for she knew that as shy as he was, he was doing this just for her, and standing right there in front of the whole audience, she became even more beautiful, if that was possible.

The music indeed was almost, as one critic wrote later, ". . . out of this world. . . ." Never had the violins and strings sounded so vibrant, the horns so brassy or woody, and the Bassoons so mellow, the chimes and xylophone so sharply struck and timbry, the harp was plucked as if from heaven, and the drums so snarey and expertly hammered. The conducting was brilliant! The audience recognizing true genius in the performance clapped and clapped after each number. The soloist had moved them from interest to enthusiasm, from laughter to tears and back again. They were so pleased that despite its terrible ordeal as well as the difficulty of the scheduled program, the whole program was being played. However, they were a bit restless and mystified by the lack of the usual intermission, (but then they did not know that Beauvena and Imppo had insisted upon this, so that no one would find out their secret.) As it was, the Manager and the Assistant Manager had tried to find out by crawling out onto the darkened stage to see just who was using the instruments. But they had to give up when they began to crawl over toes and got "shusshed." The Manager finally crawled back to where the Chief Electrician stood electrified by the song that Beauvena was singing as her fourth and final encore. He said to the enrapted listener, "Turn up the house lights, I've just got to find out where that music is coming from."

The Chief Electrician looked shocked and then began to turn purple and said, "But-t-t-t-tut-tut, we promised that we would not do that. . . ." But even as he spoke, he saw that the hall was becoming brighter and brighter. Quickly, he checked his light board to see just what had gone wrong, but all of his switches were in their proper places. "Of course," he said in disgust and anger, "it's that crazy dumb ox of an Imppo. Where's he at now, I'll short circuit him for good?" But then he too saw what it was that the audience saw and at what the Manager was staring in complete disbelief. For indeed it was Imppo himself who gave away his own secret.

Whenever she began to sing "their song," Imppo just could not keep from glowing just a little bit, in fact quite a little bit too much. Tonight was no different but then he forgot where he was, and so began to glow quite a lot, for he had seen the Love-Knot that she had tied in her hair. Thus it was that he gave away his secret, for this is what the audience saw, as the light got brighter and brighter.

There on the stage sat the unplaying players, the nonconducting conductor, but away up high behind them all on a very tall ladder sat Imppo from whom all of the very unusual light and beautiful music was coming. This was their first surprise, but the second surprise was even greater, and that was how he was making the music.

It really was all very simple. You see, as the newspapers

reported later after the concert, Imppo had very unusual horns, too. Not only because one of them could go up and down like the other one could too, or because they both could swivel around and around. But because they were hollow inside and pitted with many tiny holes. What Imppo had discovered in The Symphonic Grotto and what he was doing the night of the concert was what he had done ever since that day in the Grotto: which was to place one hand over his mouth and with the other hand pinch shut his nose, and then just blow through his horns to make the most beautiful steereophonic music ever heard. But because he was so very shy, he never before had played for any one else, except Beauvena, who right now was in the very middle of "their song" and so he dare not stop but must go right on playing with all of those in the audience watching him. So Imppo just sat there atop that very high ladder glowing and blowing, blowing and glowing, becoming brighter and brighter, sweeter and sweeter with each passing sound and moment.

And this was how Imppo a very shy young steer became the only known One Steer Symphony Orchestra in the world, simply by tooting his own horns in public, but for Beauvena.

BODY

CHAPTER TWO

The Hidden Valley

Within walking and playing distance of the home of the Three Steers, there was a very long and a very high mountain range. One mountain in particular was more towering than all of the rest: it was called, by the local Indian tribes, (in their language) "The Tower." No one knew for sure just how high it did go, for there always sat on top of it a huge billowing cloud. This cloud was called by the local Indian tribes, (in their language) "Old Thunderlesshead." Because although it always looked like it was going to thunder, it never ever did. At least, no one remembers it having done so.

This particular part of the mountain range was higher than all of the nearby mountain ranges, as well. It looked most forbidding, too. In fact, people stayed away from it. Almost all, that is. Some did not. They were never seen or heard from again.

This was the peculiar thing about "The Tower," for while it had a trail going up one of its sides, and many took it, none ever returned back down it. It was so easy to find and to climb that all of the young'uns were warned never to go near it. But some did, and they too were never seen again, ever. The local Indian Tribes called this trail (in their language) "The Up-Only Trail," because no one ever came back down it.

One fine day, Imppo and Beauvena were playing quite close to the Up-Only Trail (a bit too close really, but they were having such a good time that they did not notice this) as there were many places for play near it. When off in the distance and around a clump of cacti there came at full speed and full of "Red Eye" the Loco Weed Gang with their Leader Beau Bumly, alias, "The Bum Steer."

The sheriff and his posse were right behind them and it looked like they would be captured for sure, this time. The posse was gaining. The Loco Weed Gang was tiring. Then they spotted the two playing youngsters. At Bumly's shout, "Let's capture them. With hostages they won't dare come near us, and we'll bargain our way out," he and the gangsters as one swerved their crooked trail and headed straight for Imppo and Beauvena.

Imppo was usually on the lookout for anything that might harm Beauvena. Spotting Bumly, and although he could not hear him shout, he knew that they were coming to make trouble for him and for Beauvena. So he began to look for a safe place to run to until the sheriff could catch up with them. But there was no safe place nearby, except perhaps the Up-Only Trail. Imppo did not hesitate. Better the unknown dangers of the Up-Only Trail, than the known dangers of Bumly and the Gang. Grabbing ahold of Beauvena he began to run for the bottom of the climb.

When Bumly saw where Imppo was headed (at first he could not believe his eyes) he sped all the faster. But Imppo and Beauvena reached the trail just in time. Without hesitation, Imppo ran up the Up-Only Trail, pulling Beauvena after him. Meanwhile Bumly and The Gang were having a bitter and a losing fight with the sheriff and his posse. Bumly and some of the Gang decided that the only way to stay out of jail, was to hit the Up-Only Trail, too. So they also made a run for it. Imppo and Beauvena had by this time disappeared out of sight into Old Thunderlesshead.

The posse rounded up the remaining owlhooters, and for a long time the sheriff stood at the bottom of the Up-

Only Trail hoping against hope. Finally, even he knew in his heart that it was no use waiting any longer, so he gave the order to leave, and they set off to spread both the good and the bad news: the good, that Bumly and his Gang were no more; the bad, that Imppo and Beauvena had disappeared up the Up-Only Trail.

The sad news startled everyone almost into a stampede. Well, not everyone. For Mentoro and Bravando without saying a word to anyone left the milling herd. The last any one could remember of seeing them was about sunset near "The Tower."

Meanwhile, Imppo and Beauvena were far up the Up-Only Trail, and well into huge billowing Old Thunderless-head, where it was so foggy that neither of them could see just where the trail was and where it was not, or where it was leading them.

Imppo of course immediately turned on (and then turned up) his "Trail Light" but even with it on full power they could barely make out the next step. All he could really see was just a bare spot that looked solid enough to put down one foot. This he did. Then again. They did this for quite some time. Then the damp feeling left them and was replaced by a moving warm gentle scented draft of air, which not only dried them off, but also seemed to push-pull them along with it. It was gentle and fragrant, so much so, that they did not really notice or mind it. It was so very comforting. Also Imppo's Trail Light blinded them, at first, but soon they adjusted to it and could see about themselves.

By this time, they were well into the One-Way Tunnel. What a lovely sight met their wide-open eyes. Everywhere there grew lush green grass, towering trees, eye-catching shrubs, and flowers of every variety and color. One whole section was filled with Mangoes . . . Jasmine . . . Champak

. . . Amaranth . . . Shami, and a Rose Lotus—or was it a Lotus Rose. . . .

Brilliant sparkling lights flashed from millions of precious and semi-precious stones: diamonds, sapphires, jades, rubies, quartz, that were embedded in the ceiling like so many crystals of gigantic chandeliers. While the walls were mosaics of every kind of valuable metal: gold, silver, copper, aluminum, iron, tin and many, many others.

They wanted to stop, but could not. Perhaps, it was not just the moving air that kept them going, but also the sounds of shouting from behind them and from some of the dark openings that appeared in the Tunnel walls ever so often. Some of the voices sounded familiar. But they were not certain of this.

Suddenly, they were no longer in the Tunnel, but out into the brilliant sunlight. For a moment they could not see, but then they saw before them as far as their eyes could see a most lovely valley. Deep grass, water, and trees stretched for miles. Figures moved about in the distance. But most remarkable of all were the rainbows. For from four separate places in the valley there rose a rainbow, which went right up to Old Thunderlesshead and seemed to support it like four multicolored table legs. They walked on enchanted without realizing that they had entered into the Hidden Valley, right inside of The Tower, where all of those who took the Up-Only Trail and never returned to the outside world lived.

Meanwhile Bumly and his Gang in their frightened rush up the Up-Only Trail had gotten side-tracked into the side passageways of the One-Way Tunnel. (Their voices were some of those that Imppo and Beauvena heard.) But this was not so with Mentoro and Bravando, who of course, as soon as they heard the sheriff's story, went off to find them. They took their time searching as they went along, and so took a route much shorter. As a result all of them met at the Exit of the One Way Tunnel at the same time.

What a traffic jam that was! Bravando and Beau Bumly almost got into a fight as soon as they saw each other. But Mentoro kept them apart. But then he almost started a second "almost fight" by tripping over his long robe and bumping into one of the gansters. But because they all were in a strange land they decided to join forces and help one another. At least, until they saw where they were. Then they too entered the Hidden Valley.

Really, there is no use trying to describe the Hidden Valley. Completely, that is. But to help you imagine it, there is nothing beautiful, nothing useful, nothing that you truly need, unless it is perhaps yourself, that is missing from it. Whatever was there you wanted or could use, or thought it worthwhile. No one ever seemed to be out of things to work on, nor was there so much to be done that there was no time for relaxation. You were tired, but there always seemed to be enough energy for the chore at hand. Other writers, that you perhaps may know of, would speak of the Hidden Valley as some spoke of their Utopias, and what was that place in the Orient? But someday, you may find your way into the Hidden Valley and see it for yourself.

Eventually all of them, Imppo and Beauvena, Mentoro and Bravando, Beau Bumly and the members of the Loco Weed Gang who came with him, met. Beau and the Gang had changed. They no longer talked of going back to their old ways. Much to Bravando's surprise. Bravando too was often seen to be helping newcomers get settled. His strong muscles were appreciated. Imppo and Beauvena found many delights of their own. But the busiest person of all was Mentoro who had found in the libraries, scholars and things of the Hidden Valley so much learning that he felt like a First Grader again. Yet he is Bravando's and Imppo's older and oldest brother, and was Beauvena's Business Manager on her tour as well as being one of the smartest impresarios in the music field. But he often could walk by unrecognized, even though he may be the most learned steer in the whole world. Indeed the number of universities, colleges, and private organizations that have showered him with academic honors, awards, and rewards, is so great that not even his Mother was able after a time to keep a complete list of them all. Truly, some of the caps and gowns and hoods, which show his scholastic pedigree, have never been out of their boxes a second time. But one set of which he is so very proud—in fact he always wears it—is the very first one he ever received, that is, the one conferred upon him by his Alma Mater, Wyoming A & E (i.e., Animalism and Education). The degree (in Latin) is: STERRORIUM TALENTISSIMUS DOCTOR. The robe, which is a trifle bit too long for him and so he often trips over it, has a hood that is lined with the most beautiful silk blue ribbon ever awarded. He is often praised for his scholarship and for his voluminous writings, and he is often quoted by others. A favorite saying of his, and one that he uses either when deep in thought, or just while adjusting his eyeglasses, is: "I s'pose." This sentence, he uses to let his listeners know for sure that he is unsure about the certainty of a certain opinion held either by himself or others. Especially, some of the self-evident ones.

So excited was he about learning all about where he was, that he soon forgot where he was.

But there was one thing, a little bit of knowledge, that kept escaping him, until one day he happened to ask Beauvena about it. To his surprise everyone else in the Valley knew about it except him. What he wanted to know was: How and if one could get out of the Valley? The answer was also known to everyone: Just climb the Plaid Moonbow!

This astonished Mentoro, but what astonished him even more was that no one could climb the Moonbow. Well, this is not entirely true, for Imppo could climb it, but he never told anyone (for he was quite happy in the Hidden Valley—with Beauvena) until one day he discovered Beauvena crying and asked, "Why do you cry, Beauvena?" But this is part of another story about the three steers and before telling it, it is necessary that you know about the Symphonic Grotto, which lies just beyond Moonbow Gulch.

CHAPTER THREE

The Symphonic Grotto

The Symphonic Grotto is far down at one end of the Hidden Valley. In fact, it is just a short distance beyond Moonbow Gulch, where the Plaid Moonbow is in sight each and every night. It is in that part of the Valley where the wind seems to hold sway. Here the sandy swirls from the Friendly Desert, the cool moist breezes from the Lakes of Icy Flakes, the balmy zephyrs from the Pampered Plains, and the churning racing Up and Down Drafts from the near-by Foot Hills all meet to funnel through Moonbow Gulch and into the Symphonic Grotto, where many strange things happen to them.

All about Symphonic Grotto there are thousands upon thousands of cacti that have sprouted from just the original one hundred or so first settlers. However, the Sounding Walls are even more different. For over the centuries, the winds have carved (and even right in front of your eyes keep chiseling away) openings, shapes, forms, closings, standings, squattings, tall, short, narrow, wide, square, round, moving, not moving, slow, fast, medium, oversize, undersize, pits, pendula, and all other manner of shapes and sizes. All of which the winds play with when making the beautiful music that can always be heard in The Symphonic Grotto. Heard whenever, that is, the Winds blow, for they do not go there all of the time, but only when some one is present to listen to them play.

The Symphonic Grotto itself weaves and bends in the most fantastic ways. At times it seems to bend right around itself. There are also flying rocks: mostly small size: wood: mostly any size: and sand, all the same size, which would strike against something to make another sort of sound.

Thus from all of these things can come a lovely beautiful sound which is almost all of the time. This is why Imppo and Beauvena liked to go there so often. She had a fine singing voice, as you know. At times, it seemed that the music of the Grotto was accompanying her. This always made Imppo sit real quiet and listen with great pleasure and great delight. Never making a sound of any kind, until one horrible day when he sneezed with all of his uncontrolled might.

That particular day, Beauvena was singing for Imppo alone, as she always liked to do, when they were alone together. He, of course, could sit for hours and hours at such times and just listen. Never making even the slightest sound, sometimes not even daring to breathe for minutes upon minutes. But this day, the Winds blew his way, a tiny bit of pollen from a moonflower, or perhaps it was from a moonwort, and it tickled his nose. Then it tickled it again and again and again, until Imppo just had to sneeze. In fact he was going to sneeze. In horrified desperation he looked about for some place to hide his head, or at least his awful nose, so that when it sneezed, the noise would not interrupt Beauvena. But not a single hiding place was in sight, and then suddenly he sneezed with all of his might. But just before he did, he clamped one hand over his mouth, while with the other one he pinched tightly his nose. But neither helped. He sneezed out loud.

But instead of the loud sounding awful explosion, there came forth the sounds of two giant tubas. Then he sneezed again, and this time, it sounded just like four slide trombones. Of course what had happened was that all of the sneeze had gone up and out through the openings in his most unusual horns.

At first, he and Beauvena were so startled, that they were too startled to do anything but look startled. They stared at each other in disbelief. Then Imppo sneezed again. He could not believe his ears, or his horns. This time it sounded exactly like eight French Horns. Again and again he tooted, and each time his horns made a different sound. With Beauvena's encouragement he began experimenting and practicing and soon he could make all of the sounds that the Winds of the Symphonic Grotto could make and more. It was not too long before he and the Winds were accompanying Beauvena as she sang, and this delighted both her and him very much.

Soon they were writing music and composing words to go with it. One difficulty they had was with passers-by, who upon hearing the enchanting music would stop in to listen. At times like this Imppo would always stop playing, until they had left, for he was very shy.

The one song they both loved was the one they both called "Their Song." It was entitled: *"O, How to Climb the Moonbow"* and its words are:

VERSE ONE

> O, what I long to know
> is how to climb the Moonbow
> rising far up into the sky
> o'er mountain peaks so high.

VERSE TWO

> O, how to climb the Moonbow!
> O, how to climb the Moonbow!
> This is what I long to know!
> O, how to climb the Moonbow!

Chorus

> You'll find the missing key
> to the Moonbow's mystery
> when listening to the pounding beat
> of your heart and in your feet.

It was this song that Beauvena was singing the day she began to cry and Imppo asked, "Why do you cry?" and which led to their leaving the Hidden Valley.

CHAPTER FOUR

The Plaid Moonbow

In order to leave the Hidden Valley, it was necessary, as you already know, to climb The Plaid Moonbow. The real problem was, how to climb a Moonbow. How and where was one to get a foothold, or a hand hold, if that was the way? Many had tried, but not one was ever able to get more than one foot off of the ground in the attempt. That is until Imppo came along.

Much later Mentoro would try to explain to them just how it was possible to climb a Moonbow. He used some long difficult sounding scientific words, like: it was all possible because of the moon's diameter of 2,160 miles; along with its mean distance from Moonbow Gulch of about 238,857 miles; and the sympathetic solid-state matching light wave measured steps that Imppo was able to radiate, and the added fact that water and dust are both solid matter. But what happened was this.

Imppo and the others gathered at the bottom of the Plaid Moonbow. (Bravando did not like the idea of taking along Beau Bumly and some of his old Gang, but Imppo had insisted.)

While they stood there waiting for just the right moment of the new moonlight, Imppo explained again just what they must do. The most important thing was for them to hold tightly onto each other's hands (to the one ahead of them and to the one behind them) otherwise they would fall to earth, just like mountain climbers sometimes do, when their ropes break. The next thing was to be sure and step exactly where he placed his own feet. Otherwise, they would fall right through the colors of the Plaid Moonbow. Finally, he asked again for the hundredth time, "Do you really want to leave?" For it was a dangerous journey, not only the climb up, but where they might come down. He could not guarantee where they would come back to solid earth. But all agreed, especially Beauvena, that they wanted to leave the Hidden Valley. So the climb began, that is, after Imppo made certain that all were holding onto each other's hands. Beauvena came next after him, then Mentoro, Beau and the others. Last of all, was Bravando, who was watchful just in case someone did fall. He might be able to catch them. But no one did.

Soon they were inside of Old Thunderlesshead. Inside the silvery billowing foggy cloud, the slow climb became even more dangerous and they had to watch their step very carefully, for the colors began to run wherever and whenever they were watery and soft from the dampness. At other times, they could barely see, and surely some of them would have fallen except for Imppo's warning, "To hold tightly onto each other." Mentoro had great difficulty, for he could not reach down to lift up the bottom of his too long robe and so forever kept tripping over it from time to time. Also, he had to quit trying to adjust his eyeglasses as they slid down on his nose, but even if he could have, it would not have helped too much, since they were all misty and foggy from the dampness of the cloud, and so he would not be able to see through them.

Then quite suddenly without their realizing it, the foggy dampness blew away and they were on solid earth, again. They were out of the cloud. But where were they, now? None of them knew at first. (For a fact, as they found out later they were in the Orient, just as Imppo had warned them they might be when they came back down to earth. But this is where they met the Oriental Philosopher, Il Yo-Tse.)

CHAPTER FIVE

The Oriental Philosopher

There was something very special and wonderful about being back in their own real world, again. Soon they discovered just where they were. They were in the Far East. In fact, they were half-way around the world from their western home. It was just as easy for them to go one way as it was for them to go the other way. Unless of course they went North or South, and Mentoro, who was one steer who could steer by the stars, made certain they did not do either of these.

Mentoro fortunately for them all had taken courses in most of the languages they would need (some he also learned while in the Hidden Valley). Now and again he would stop to talk with just anyone. He discovered the shortest route home, but it was to be a long time before they reached home and the family reunion.

What delayed them were little panels that they kept seeing along the way. Always there was some very wise saying on them. But what attracted them most was always the last panel. It was blank and shiny. Nothing on it at all. Nothing, that is, unless you got up real close, then, all you saw was your own face staring right back at you. Once in a while, it looked back at you as if to say, "I understood, why didn't you?" Very inscrutable, these oriental blank shiny panels.

Some of the sayings that the group liked more than others were written down by Mentoro. This one had six panels with of course the sixth being blank and shiny.

> *Has any flower ever bloomed*
> *Without stem or roots,*
> *Soil, or weather,*
> *Or the care of a gardener?*
> *And what of the weeds?*

This one had seven panels, the last one blank and shiny.

> *For the eyes*
> *To lose their sight*
> *Is a tragedy, but*
> *For the heart*
> *To lose its insight*
> *That is tragic.*

Mentoro became more and more interested in these sayings and especially in finding out who it was that was their author, or who thought enough of them to put them up. But the more he searched the less he could find out. About all anyone knew was that one day the signs were not there. The next day they were there. Who put them up no one seemed to know. In fact no one had seen any of the signs being put up. The local Orientals simply referred to whoever it was, as "The Oriental Philosopher."

Finally one day Mentoro announced that he must go in search of The Oriental Philosopher. After much discussion the little group decided to go with Mentoro in his search. That is all, except Beau and his gang, who said that they were heading back home, and no longer walked with them. Bravando was not too sorry to see them go.

They searched far and wide, high and low, but could not find "the putter upper of the signs," as Mentoro began to call their elusive Oriental. Still they searched on day after day. Finally, one warm spring day, they came to another of the many crossroads at which they had to choose a new direction of travel.

Mentoro was unwilling to go on without first discussing again once more whether or not the others wished to head for home. He was reluctant to leave without having found his friend (for now that is how he thought of the Oriental Philosopher). It was a warm balmy day and as they sat and talked in the quiet fragrant shade of a blossoming cherry tree, one by one they drifted off to restful sleep. While they slept, a figure came along the opposite roadway, and just across from the sleeping group began to put up little signs, tapping each into the ground with a small silver hammer.

Mentoro awoke with a sense of urgency about him. It was almost as if he dared not sleep again. He did not know at first just why he felt that way. But he could not keep his eyes shut, no matter how hard he tried to close them again. Then he heard the gentle hammering and sat up to see what it was and who was making that noise on such a quiet restful afternoon to disturb him on his bed of leaves.

His stirring had caused the others to awaken, too. Bravando was the next to notice the working figure across the way. Mentoro was watching quietly and seemed to be waiting for something else more important. Then the last sign appeared. It was a blank shiny one. It must be! It had to be The Oriental Philosopher, and it was, of course. Scrambling to his feet Mentoro read the saying of the signs, as he trippingly started across the roadway towards the waiting figure that stood quietly as he approached nearer:

> *The same pathway*
> *Between the homes*
> *Of neighbors*
> *Is for both*

> *Just as winding,*
> *Just as long,*
> *Just as rough*
> *But where it may for one*
> *Be all downhill,*
> *Then it must for the other*
> *Be an Uphill climb.*

"It must . . ." Imppo started to say but Beauvena gently placed her hand on his arm to quiet him, lest he disturb them, and nodded her lovely head that she too understood that they had at last found the Oriental Philosopher.

Mentoro meanwhile crossed over (tripping a little bit as he walked too rapidly) and began to speak with the waiting Il Yo-Tse (for this was the name of The Oriental Philosopher).

Later, Imppo was never quite sure just who joined whom. But they all began to travel together throughout the country, and putting up little signs as they went. Always taking roads however that never led homewards. The two scholars were lost in their own thoughts most of the time. But Il Yo-Tse was greatly taken up with Bravando's great size and strength (for he could drive a sign post into the ground, no matter how hard, with just one mighty blow). Beauvena's printing of the signs was much, much nicer. Yet it was with Imppo that Il Yo-Tse liked to spend spare moments, listening to him make music, or accompany Beauvena as she sang. Often times, Imppo would play among the flowers, changing color as he went from one to the other: very much like a chameleon can do. Also his Night Light was of great help when they wished to put up signs at night secretly. While his Trail Light proved itself time and again when in strange places.

Most of the time, Mentoro and Il Yo-Tse just talked.

They also began to make up sayings together. Before long Il Yo-Tse would suggest a first line (and panel) and wait for Mentoro to think of the next, and so on. Like: Il Yo-Tse: Whatever you are, be it. Mentoro: Whatever your neighbor is, let him be it. Il Yo-Tse: Never be unkind. Mentoro: Never be untruthful. Il Yo-Tse: Always be interested and curious. Mentoro: Never be afraid to fail.

Then of course Il Yo-Tse always insisted on the blank shiny panel.

There are other examples of what they did together, like this one Beauvena liked so well:

> *Truly, the heart*
> *May not weep or smile,*
> *But then the eyes and lips*
> *Do they really know*
> *Happiness or sadness?*

(and of course the blank shiny panel).

Once in a while they would relax from their work, and compose poetry for each other's criticism. Bravando liked this one (because, as he said, he could not understand it):

> *Beginning another like whether*
> *I AM to stand*
> *with beginning or to with-*
> *stand beginning since so*
> *often at here the failure and*
> *not always at the ending long*
> *after each successive NOW of*
> *real TIME gives subSTANCE*
> *of the preSENT to a spawned*
> *torture growing mosaic fashion into*
> *the impending all*
> *ways here integrated frus-*
> *tration fa-I-L-U-re The End.*

Imppo liked a different one (one that he could understand, as he said) :

> *Once, a Giant Pigmy*
> *with a livid eye lived nearby.*
> *"A Giant Pigmy with a*
> *livid eye," so they said, "is*
> *mean." And then each son*
> *handed on this truth to*
> *each father. Yet fancy this,*
> *this Pigmy Giant is*
> *kind. So kind in fact,*
> *that the eye became livid*
> *from blinking against all*
> *who said, "A Giant Pigmy*
> *with a livid eye*
> *is mean."*

At times like this, the two Friends needed no blank shiny panel, but could just look into each other's eyes and heart. Some signs, however, they would discuss with the little group before putting them up, like this one:

> *Love without*
> *Communication*
> *Is like a soul without*
> *A body, and thus are*
> *The lonely without*
> *Visitors.*

By now many months had passed and with each new moon, the Friends knew that soon they must part company. Finally, they again came to a crossroads. This time, they all knew that it would separate them. After a brief, "Good-by," Imppo and Beauvena walked on ahead down the road they must take homeward. Bravando followed in a moment. Only Mentoro remained behind with Il Yo-Tse. But only for a moment.

The two old Friends stood there in the middle of the crossroads speaking quietly. Then Il Yo-Tse spoke to Mentoro. Spoke very much like a Teacher giving a final instruction and examination to a Favorite Student. Il Yo-Tse said:

"Life, Mentoro, knows no death." And waited for Mentoro to answer, which he did without hesitation:

"As Love, Il Yo-Tse, knows no birth."

For a moment longer each looked deep into the other's eyes and heart. Then Il Yo-Tse bowed very deeply to Mentoro, who also bowed with great respect. Both then looked once more, turned from the other and began walking down their chosen road, away from each other.

The little group at first could not bring itself to turn and look back, but then it did, for just a glance. Imppo later said to Beauvena how much the disappearing figure looked like a tired farmer going in from the fields after a hard day's work, but heading homeward. Beauvena said it reminded her of a weary mother closing her tired eyes to sleep at last, yet keeping her ears wide awake for any troubled cries from her resting family.

CHAPTER SIX

The Return Home

The travelers were again unsure of their exact location. (They had been trying to find a relative nearby.) When a white cow walked into view, Bravando was all for going over and asking where they were. But Mentoro quickly stopped him from doing so, and said, "That's a Sacred Cow, Bravando, and we must not disturb her. In fact, she is untouchable." At this, frowns appeared upon the brows of Imppo and Beauvena. Mentoro noticed and asked what was wrong.

"I always thought," said Imppo, "that the 'untouchables' were something quite different."

Mentoro thought a moment then said, "You're right, Imppo, but these are also untouchable." And he began to explain the difference and meaning of each. Meanwhile, the heifer rambled away up to her lovely ankles in white-dust.

The little group moved on, as Imppo continued to shake his head with doubt and lack of understanding. Beauvena, too, shook her head and glanced at the very shy Imppo. But at least they now knew where they were. Home was nearer than before, but it would be many moons before they would arrive in time for the family reunion.

Since they were abroad, both Mentoro and Bravando were very much interested in finding out as much as they could about their ancestors, so they took time to look up some of them. A couple of "tips" took them away off their route and delayed them, like the ones: that sent them looking for a Papal Bull; or trying to locate one relative who was said to be a very active trader in the world's largest bull market; or the one, when they called at No. 10 to see, "Sir John Bull," and were turned away unceremoniously. As they were leaving, Bravando accidentally (or was it?) bumped into an English Bulldog, who growled back, "If you want a fight, why don't you go across the channel, where they've got some real bullfighters your size." This, of course, was like waving a red flag in front of Bravando, and for days he would talk of nothing else, except going across the channel. Finally, the little group, realizing that he was becoming quite "bull-headed" about the whole idea, gave in to him.

Now about Bravando, he would never ever be mistaken for Mentoro's brother, but he could be related to younger Imppo. For he, Bravando, stopped going to school almost before he started going. They never could corral him long enough to break that wild streak which appeared every so often: ("After his Father," said his Mother); ("After his Mother," said his Father.) But he was not all wildness. He would for example listen very carefully and respectfully to "Menty," as he liked to call The Professor, which is another of Mentoro's titles. Also he could ask some very difficult questions, like: "Why is water wet, rather than dry?" Nevertheless, he was better known for his huge size, tremendous strength, and his graceful way of moving about, for you would never worry about his being in a China shop, alone. That he was as strong as a bull, no one doubted, and only a few jealous ones, like Bumly, ever doubted that he was the strongest bull in the whole world.

Bravando also had the two longest, pointedest, and most majestic horns ever measured. These, of course, were very useful in a fight—of which he had many, but never lost any —for he could parry and thrust with the beauty of the murderous skill of a champion swordsman going home for the kill.

Yet what pleased his Mother (and a herd of female admirers) was his soft shiny, silky, inky, ebony hide, which cannot be described in words. To believe its breath-taking beauty, you must see—or try to see it on a really dark night, for at times even with his Night Light "ON" and with Bravando standing right in front of him, Imppo would not see him and would bump into one of Bravando's dark slab-like, iron-like sides. Of course these too along with his two fierce horns were of great help in a fight—of which he had many, but never lost any.

Yet do not misunderstand about Bravando, for in spite of his gigantic size, unmatched strength, and heavy weight, he is quite gentle. Except when riled! And now, he was riled!

After a rough crossing, they left the boat and were met by the American Consul. Upon finding out just why they had come, he remarked to himself, "That's almost like carrying coals to Newcastle." But when he saw the great interest that the Managers of the leading arenas and bullfighters displayed in Bravando's size, strength, and especially, his intelligence, he was not so sure.

All of the managers stormed around Bravando and Mentoro (who was trying to act as Bravando's Manager, who was fast becoming impatient with all this talking). Each Manager claimed to have the number one bullfighter under contract. Finally, when he could stand no more of this petty bickering, Bravando said flatly, "I'll meet them all, at once, on the same day, same time, in the same bullring," and then walked out.

His remark was met with a stunned silence from all, except Mentoro, and the Bull Ring Managers, who could just picture the overflow crowd that would attend such a fantastic event. It truly would be la fiesta bravissima! the fight of the century. After much haggling, the place, time and the special rules were set. The bullfighters' managers all left. The arena managers all left. Mentoro left to find a hospital with a bed large enough for Bravando, "just in case."

The signs in the Plaza de Toros showed that the very best of the world's bullfighters were there for the occasion. Masterful Matadors, Terrifying Toreadors, Reigning Rejoneadors, and the Pick of Picadors. All had been arriving for hours with each being greeted with shouts of praise. This was Bravando's first look at them, and he began to realize just what he had gotten himself into. Mentoro had tried to explain it to him, but at the time he just would not listen to anyone.

Aficionados and novillos and tourists had arrived in such large numbers that the arena was crowded beyond its capacity. All the local bulls wanted to fill Bravando in on the different techniques and moves of the various bullfighters, but he soon was so confused by their well-meant advice, that he asked all of them to stop trying to help him. Beauvena made certain that he looked his very best. Mentoro tried to get him to rest just before going into the ring, but Bravando would have no part of it and only paced back and forth in the bull pen awaiting his turn as he was always nervous before a fight—of which he had many but never lost any—yet.

Bravando had been scheduled for the Main Event, after a couple of brief "warm up" fights for the other bullfighters. Once in the ring, he would be all right, for it's always that way before a fight. Right now he was nervous, because he hadn't counted on just *that* kind of a bullfighter. He had misunderstood. But if they were bullfighters, well, so was he. If they were the best, well, he was better than they were. But we'll see in a few minutes. He had no doubts about who would win, however. But, it was just that they kept carrying bulls out of the ring. Some badly bruised or seriously hurt. Others had a sword or a lance sticking in them. This rather un-nerved him a bit. But if that was the way they wanted to fight, why he was ready with his long sharp horns. Finally, his moment of truth came. It was time to go into the arena. With a look of confidence at his friends, he walked through the open gates and into the vast ring.

At first, the sounds of the shouting, and the blasts of the trumpets, startled him. Also the many colors and moving figures dazzled him. But only for a moment. Then he saw coming at him the vast army of bullfighters, and he felt better. After a good careful look at it, he lowered his head and charged straight into the middle of the flower of bull-fighters.

There is no need to describe in full gory details that bloody afternoon, and the blows and counterblows, the feignings and faintings, the "Oles" and the "Ouches," the flailing arms or legs and flying flails, the sailing caps and flapping capes, the passes and the passings of Matadors, Picadors and Toreadors, of the painful red tears and the salty eye swelling tears, and the swirling sand storm that soon hid the furious artful battle from everyone's sight. Every so often from out of this sand cyclone in the middle of the arena would come a bullfighter or two or three sailing through the air to land in a senseless heap. Then nothing came out of the cloud of sand. All was quiet, except the swishing sands. Quietly it began to settle to the arena floor, and the crowd began to see once more.

All around the arena were the very best Matadors, Torea-dors, and Rejoneadors, lying in piles and heaps here and there. Debris and litter was in profusion like confetti. But right in the middle of it all there stood straight and very tall, bloodied and bruised, one magnificent unbeaten unbowed bullfighter, Bravando. Truly, now, he was "Numero Uno."

A stunned silence greeted his appearance. Then the crowd with a good show of true sportsmanship went wild with "Oles" for a true champion. His first words, "Who's next?" brought even greater and louder shouts of "Oles" and "El Toro bravissimo," "El Toro Magnifico," and sweetest of all, "El Toro Numero Uno."

When no more bullfighters stepped forward, Bravando began to wonder about what to do next. Perhaps he should be given some sort of award or trophy, so he could show the family back home. Especially, Bumly. So in his deep thunderous voice (like a bull horn) he said, "If there are any, I'll take my prizes now and leave."

The yelling crowd, the moaning bullfighters (and the nearby bulls) were shocked into a stunned silence, hardly daring to breathe. In fact, the loudest noise was that of the last tiny grain of sand gently falling to the floor of the arena. The crowd stood perfectly still. The bullfighters trembled even more. The nearby bulls all leaned forward to see what the Manager of the Arena would do, now. For they all knew perfectly well what the usual prizes were that went to the winner of any bull fight. Especially one who had fought so skillfully as Bravando. But did he really want them? But he had won, hadn't he! He was entitled to the trophies. The Manager had not counted on this sudden turn of events and did not know quite what to do. He went over to Mentoro and whispered into his ear. The two of them whispered together. Then they walked into the ring towards the waiting Bravando. Mentoro went along "just in case." The crowd, the bullfighters, and the nearby bulls all watched breathlessly as he neared the waiting Bravando.

Bravando couldn't believe his own ears, when the Manager told his sad tale. What was it that he had won! As trophies! For a moment, he stood there very much alone with his thoughts. Then with an artful mighty thrust of his longest sharpest horn he speared a cape lying nearby, and said in his most thunderous tones, "I'll just take this for a souvenir," and began walking from the arena. Truly a bullfighter's bullfighter.

CHAPTER SEVEN

The Ancestors

The local American Ambassador, who personally saw them off, had made certain that the quartet rode first class on the fastest first cattle boat heading home. Thus with a special concert here and there, a look in on the bull market, an attempted kidnapping—the one staged by Beau Bumly, and a few more adventures, they all arrived home in time for the family reunion.

Open hearts and warm hearths greeted their return home. No one had expected to see them ever again. (The little group said nothing about how they left The Hidden Valley, except to say that Imppo had discovered a way.)

Now, it was their family's custom to gather and celebrate the birthday of The Lamb, so all were present to greet them, and to listen to the family's history, which was retold each year on this occasion. However, when it came time to read from the family's precious Book, it was given, not as usual to the oldest member present, for this time all had quietly agreed that Mentoro should have the honor. There was something different about him, since he had gone away looking for Imppo and Beauvena. Also, he looked like he had something that he wanted to say to them. Truly, he did, for he not only read from the family's history, but also added new and unknown facts from time to time.

He spoke of how long ago, some branches of the family had often offered their lives; their blood and their ashes as a sacred sacrifice. How at times they were misunderstood and misused, and even idolized for their great strength.

Even becoming symbols for Strength and for Life-giving Forces. He wisely pointed out that their family's coat-of-arms showed not only the mark of atonement, but also the blood red field of love.

But with the birth of the Lamb (and one of their ancestors had been there in the stable that night, and passed on the information, as that of an eye witness) this ancient honorable custom in some places and for some had come to a stop. Yet not for all. Many still clung to cherished and revered traditions, of which they had seen some on their way home.

He spoke of many other things, and the time passed rapidly from eve to the approaching dawn. Bravando had sat quietly nearby Mentoro listening. Finally, Mentoro handed him the heavier Book, so that one strong enough to hold it might carry it back to its place of honor in their Father's house.

Mentoro stood up and with a few quiet words of "Goodbye" to his parents, walked towards the door, opened it and went outside, leaving the door ajar. Bravando began to follow him . . . Imppo and Beauvena also went after him. For they knew, although nothing had been said, that Mentoro was going in search of his old friend, Il Yo-Tse.

CONCLUSION

CHAPTER EIGHT

The Happy Ending

Outside, Mentoro walked on towards the rising sun, which was still below the eastern horizon that was just now showing the first light of a new dawn. Hearing Bravando, Imppo and Beauvena behind him, he waited for them to catch up. Nothing was said at first as they walked a little ways together. It was taken for granted that he would go back, once they reached home. The three waited for him to speak.

Mentoro began to speak of much the same as before, and of other things brothers do in such parting moments. Beauvena listened quietly while continuing to hold tightly onto Imppo's hand (and surprisingly enough, as when they climbed the Moonbow, he did not glow even a little bit). Mentoro had noticed for some time how they were always making calf-eyes at each other.

He spoke of other things as well, but he also spoke of Love. Of Lovers. Perhaps, because of the family reunion. Or Imppo and Beauvena. Or maybe just for Bravando. Or just thinking out loud.

Some of the many things he said they had heard before. Others they knew from their own hearts. But perhaps it was just the way he said it, his attitude that made it so very much different this time. So much clearer. It might have been only the moment itself, for now truly they were listening.

When Mentoro spoke of love, its different kinds, and of its importance, they listened carefully for they knew then that he was about to leave them. Imppo was especially attentive to the part about ". . . that it is impossible to understand completely and perfectly . . . all that there is to know . . . why not even all of the world's very best poets, writers, scientists, believers or non-believers, nor even the best philosophers knew all. . . ." So thought Imppo, "Why should I expect to know all . . . and yet why shouldn't I know enough. . . ."

Bravando too listened very carefully to what "Menty" was saying, ". . . truly the greatest sacrifice one can make for a loved one is to give up one's own life . . . that's one's all . . . but never doubt that sometimes such a sacrifice is far easier than the one that comes anew with each new moment of time and life . . . demanding that very same sacrifice . . . made just a moment before . . . once again . . . and with never a final 'all' . . . but always a new demand for the same one, just as before. . . ."

Beauvena understood much better when Mentoro remarked, ". . . that when their first ancestor complained about being alone . . . because of the fact that there was not one other of his own kind about him. . . . He could have given him a brother, but He did not do so, because He had something else in Mind . . . and not just the founding of families either . . . although this is very important . . . for what had helped our first ancestor to become so lonesome was also his great learning, as well as his greater yearning . . . he knew everything about him that he had to know . . . there wasn't anything he didn't know . . . then He saw that He had not put into his world two important things . . . that were important about Himself . . . not only had He left out mystery . . . but also He had not given him someone to love and to return freely an equal love . . . and thus all of the Beauvenas are here so that all of the Imppos might not only have someone to love and be loved by . . . but also to have mystery in their lives . . . for every person knows that they never have figured them out. . . ."

They understood a bit better, when he added finally, ". . . long ago someone else I s'pose, wrote that we all know with what effort and how far a lover will go to meet a beloved. . . . How much more then will the lover of wisdom be tempted to go in search of his heavenly mistress. . . ."

Mentoro talked on for a little while then fell silent. It was time to say goodbye. Imppo and Beauvena were the first to leave, and both Mentoro and Bravando watched as they walked westward towards the towering mountain. Mentoro knew they would live happily ever after. About Bravando, he was not so sure.

The two of them spoke for a little while longer, then without so much as a final look or parting word, Mentoro began walking eastwards towards the now visible sun.

For a time, Bravando stood there uncertain as just what to do, which way to turn. He looked off in the direction Imppo and Beauvena had taken. Then after Mentoro. For a long moment he bowed his head, as if in quiet meditation, then he too turned and began walking.

This is all that is known about The Three Steers. And Beauvena, Beau Bumly and The Loco Weed Gang. But of this you may be certain. Bravando, too, found happiness, as the Reader of any Fairy-Philosophical Tale should know, he would.

A Post-Quote:

"... A symbol, for Lonergan, has a very precise meaning—it is an image of a real or imaginary object that evokes a feeling or is evoked by a feeling. Symbols are the primordial expression of that affectivity and aggressivity that relate us to our worlds of meaning. They express and reveal our fundamental attitude, stance, orientation towards that world. ..."